Vol 4

MAZE

FOR KIDS

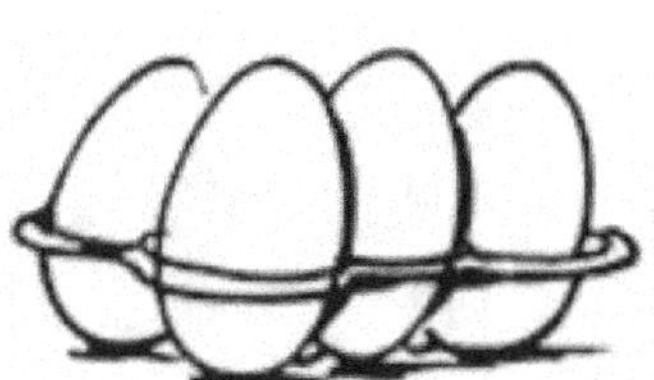

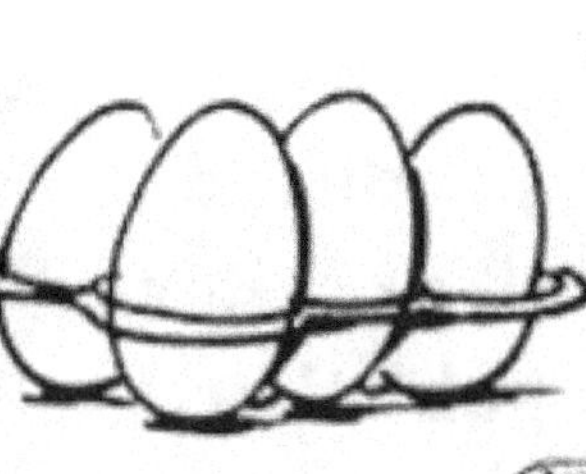

MAZE BOOK

SOCIAL MEDIA

(f) /MySweetBooks1

(t) /MySweetBooks1

(i) /MySweetBooks1

(p) /MySweetBooks

Email Us : mysweetbooks1@gmail.com

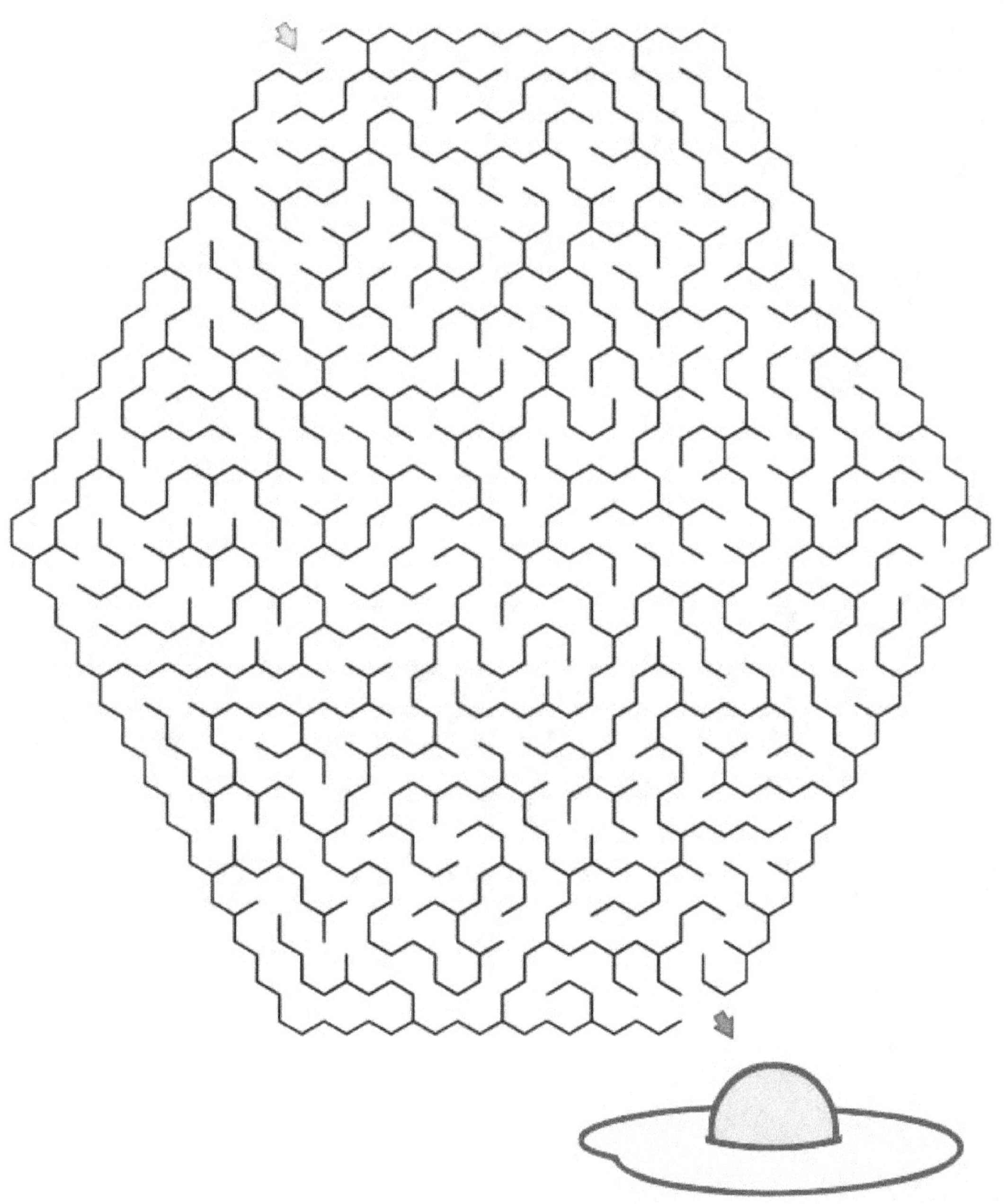

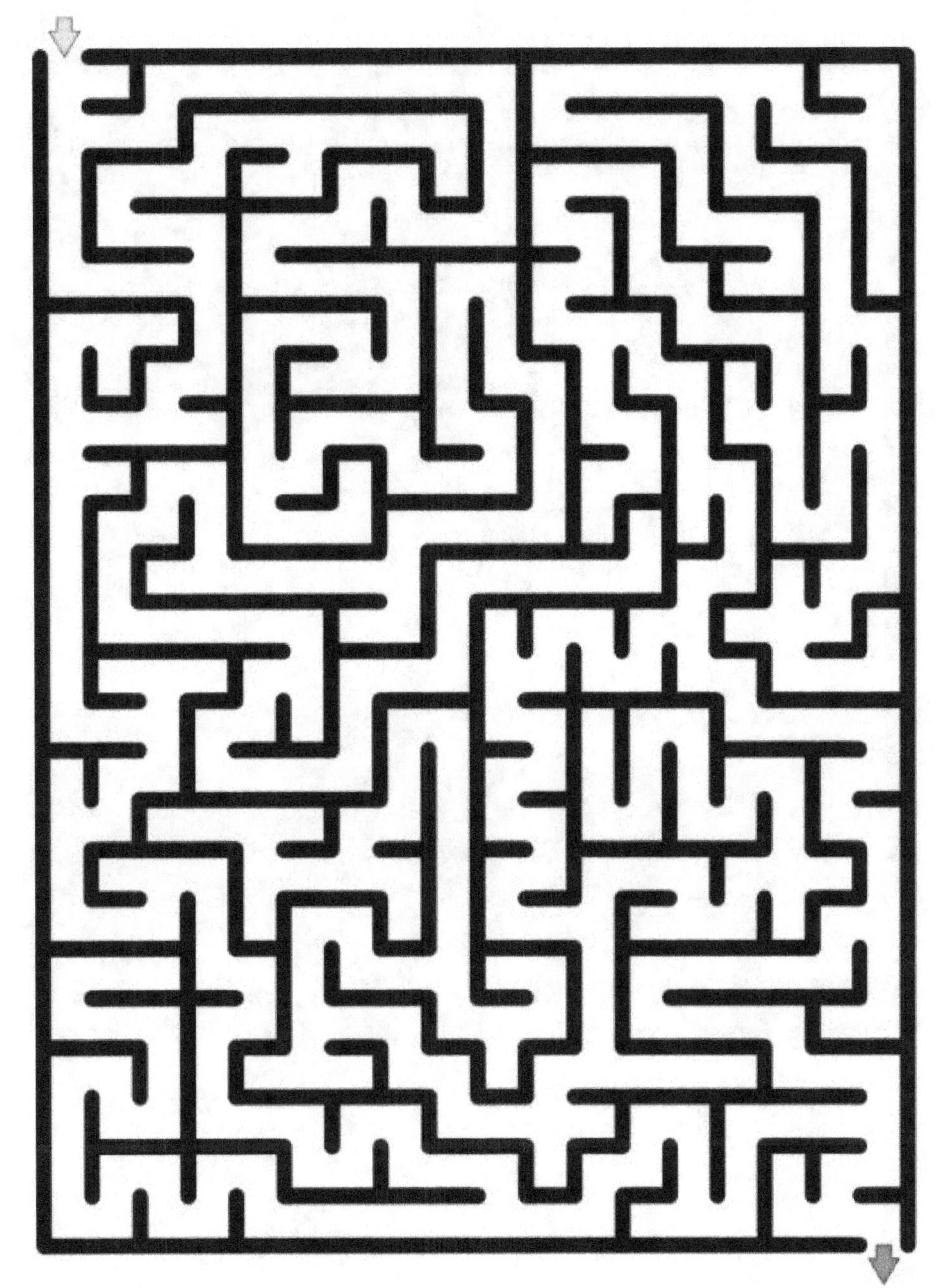

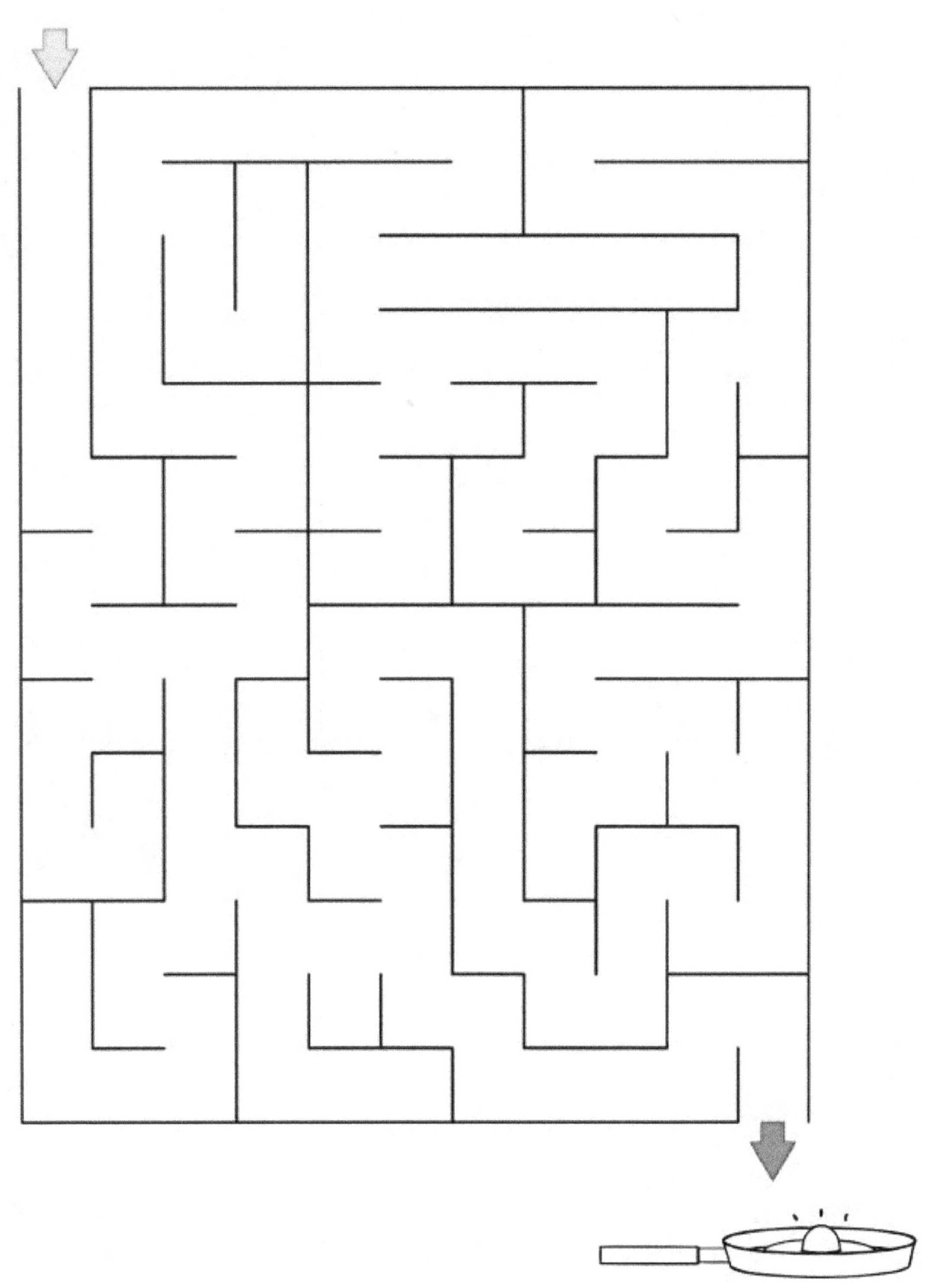

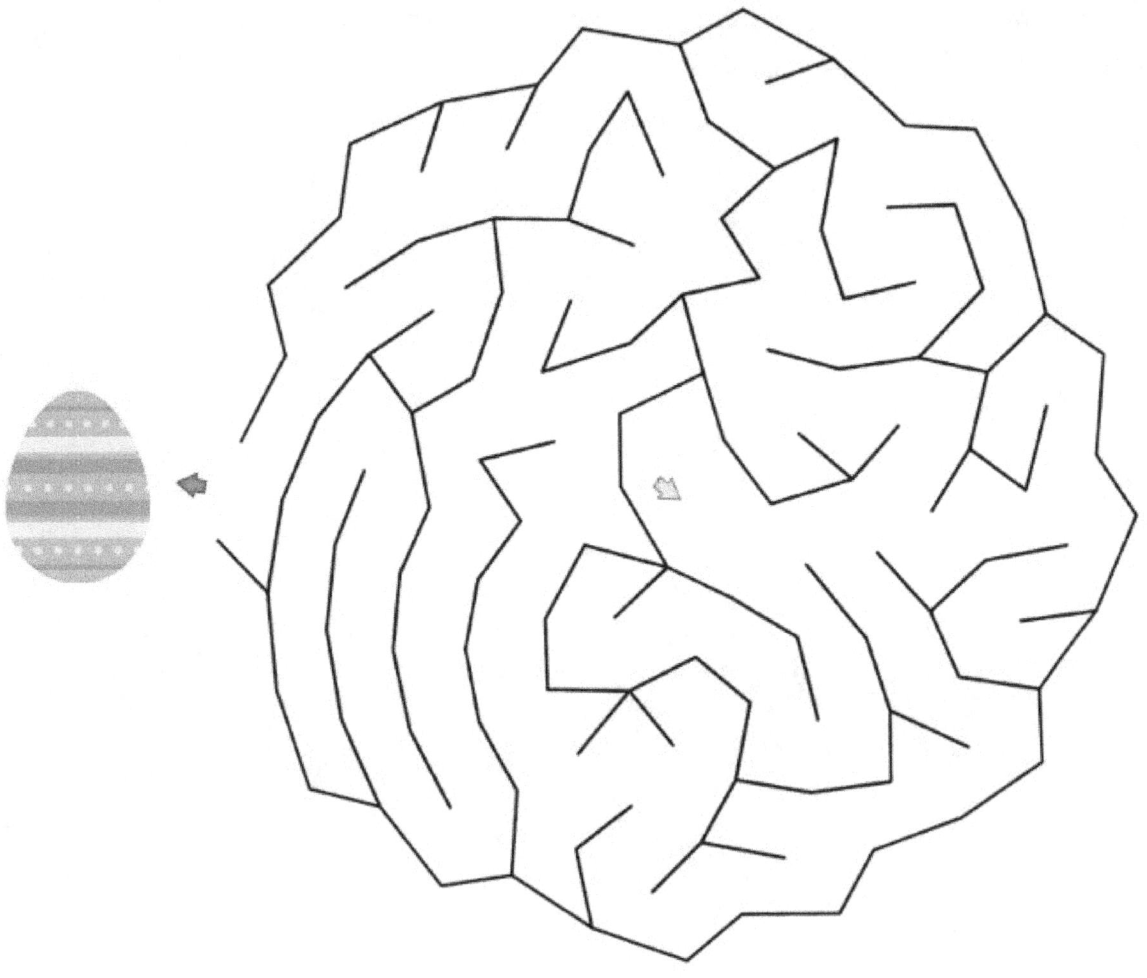

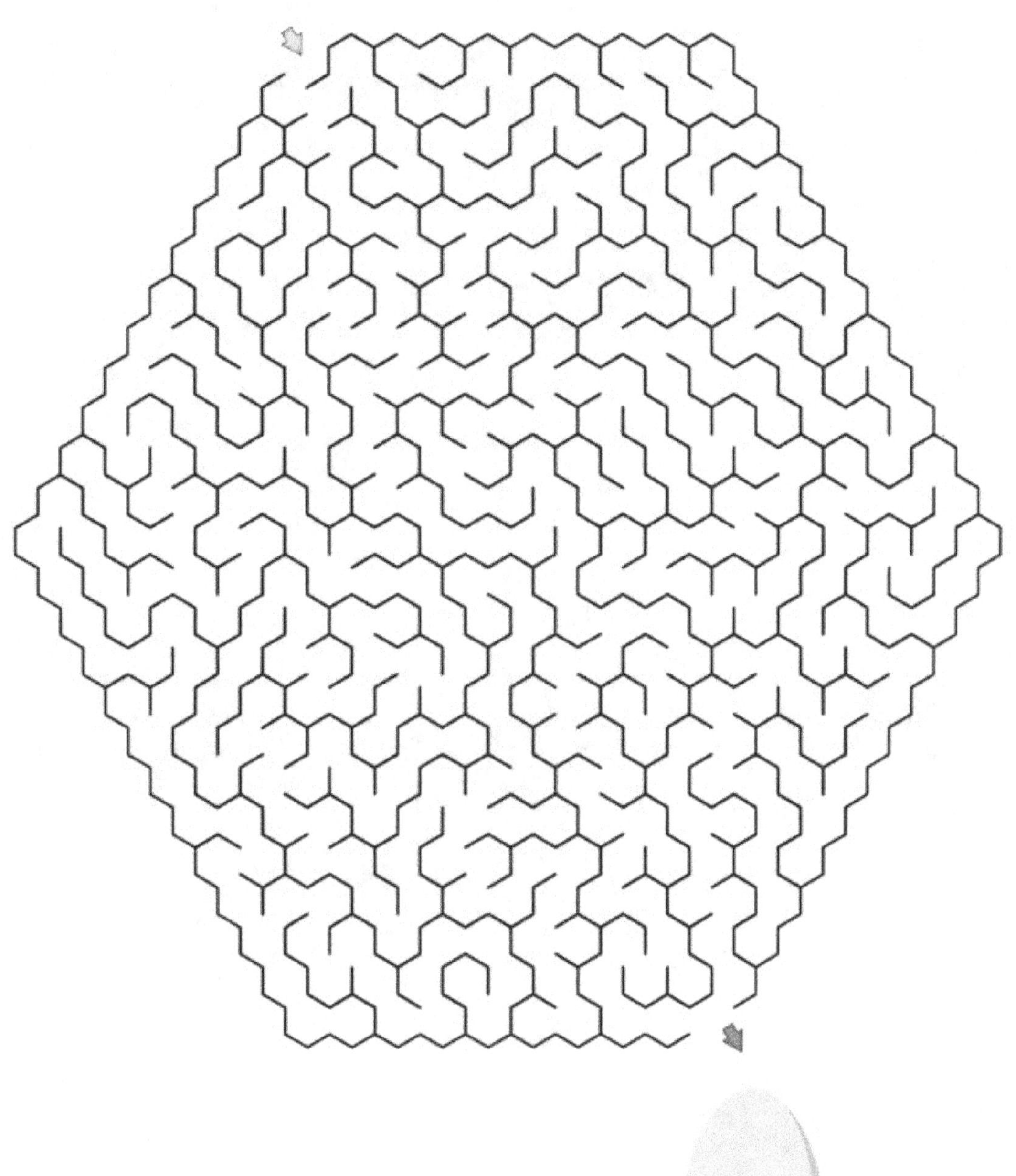

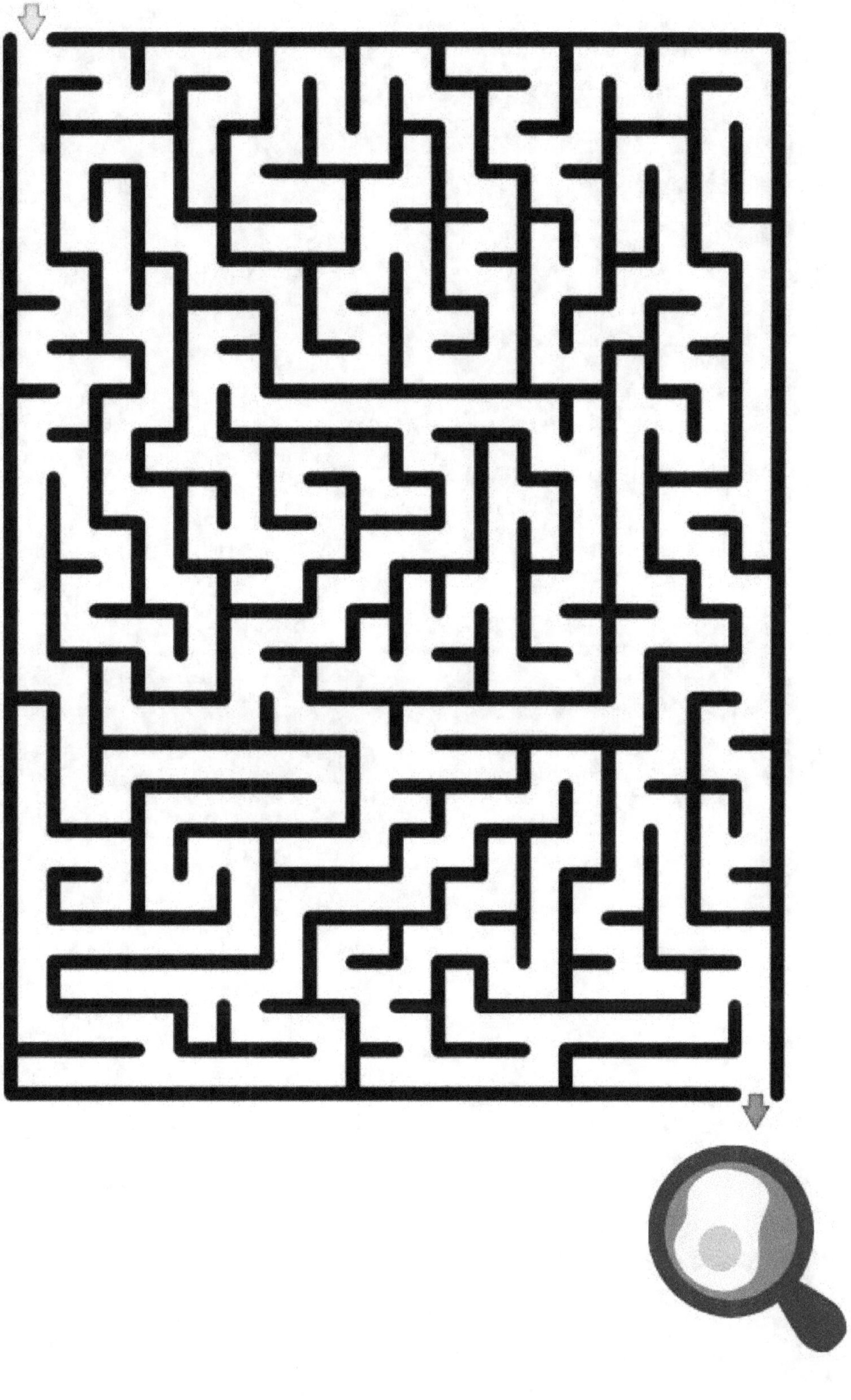

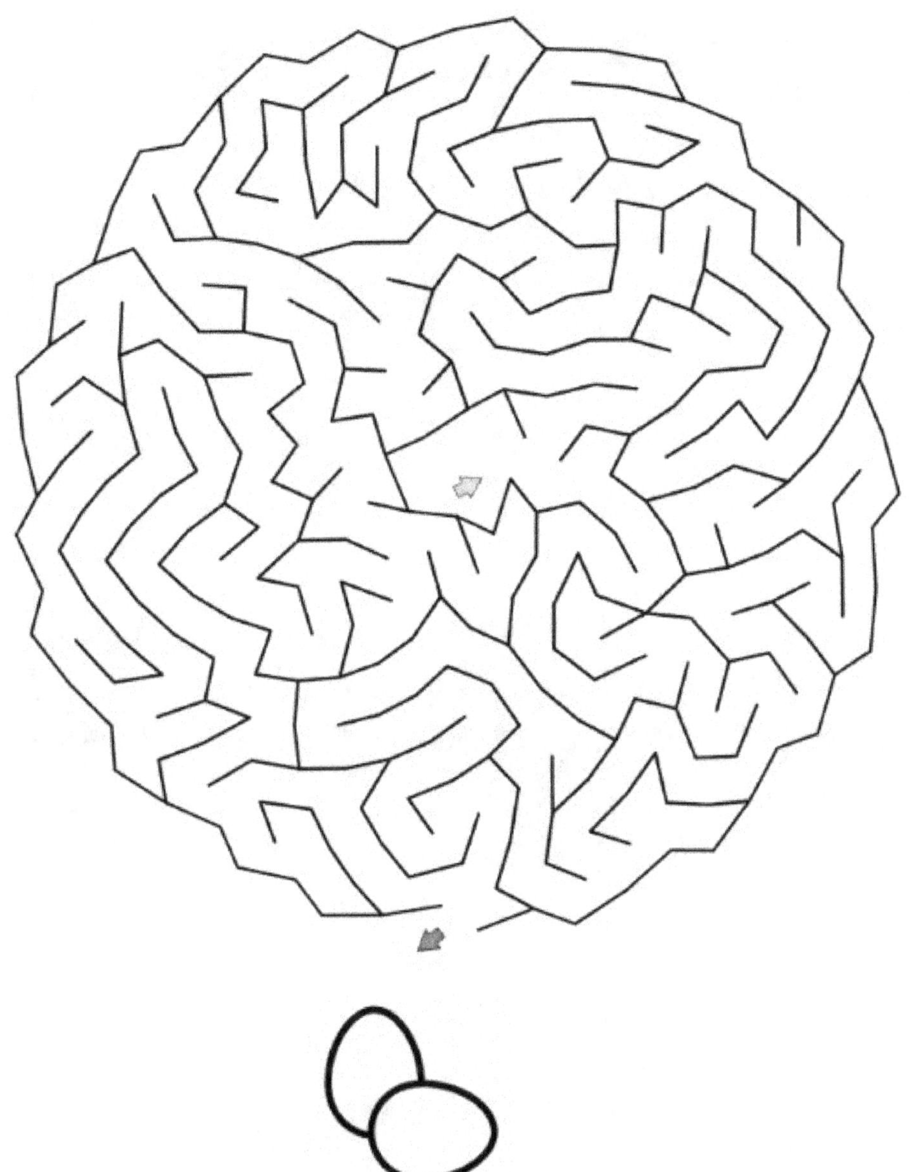

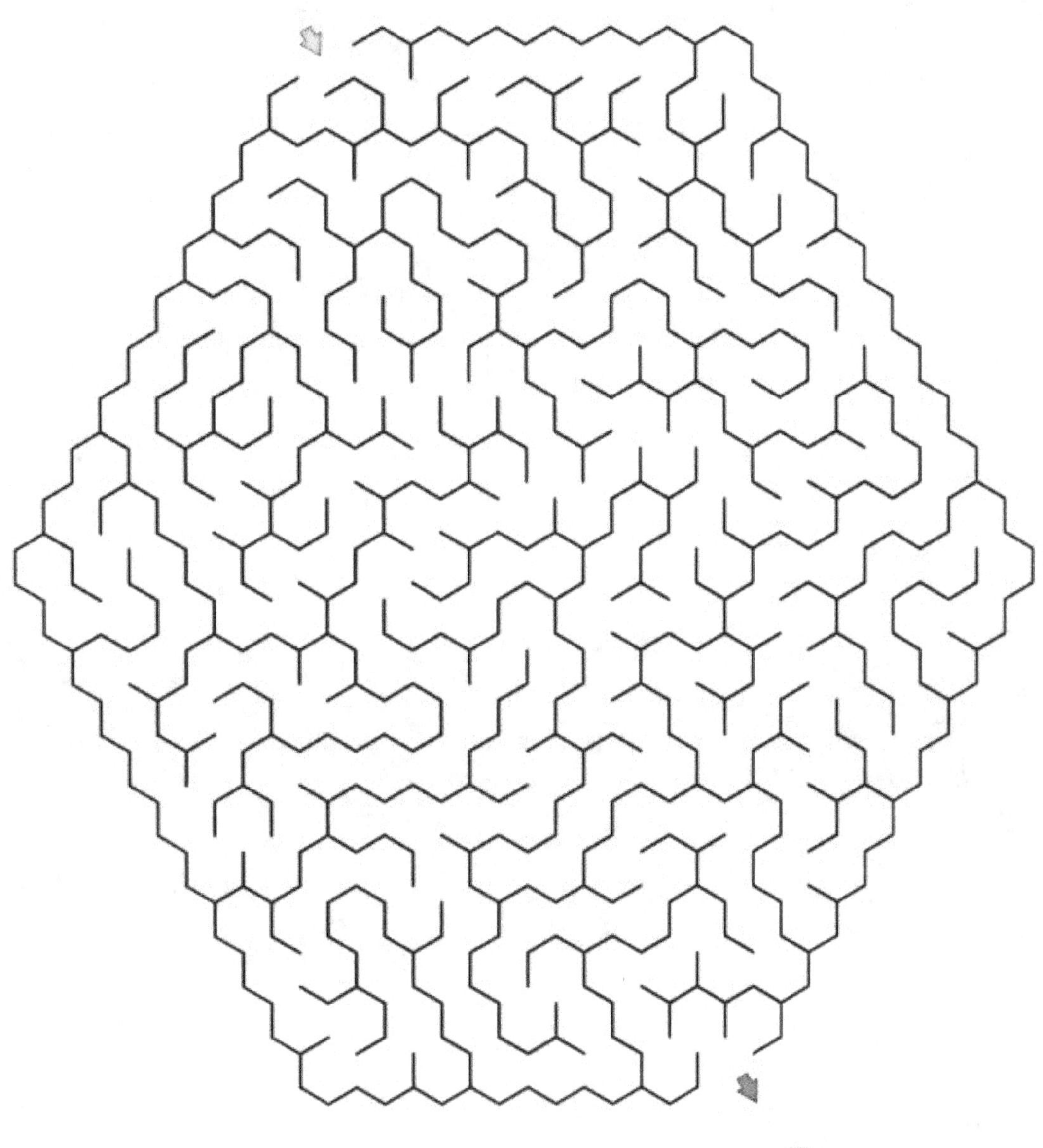

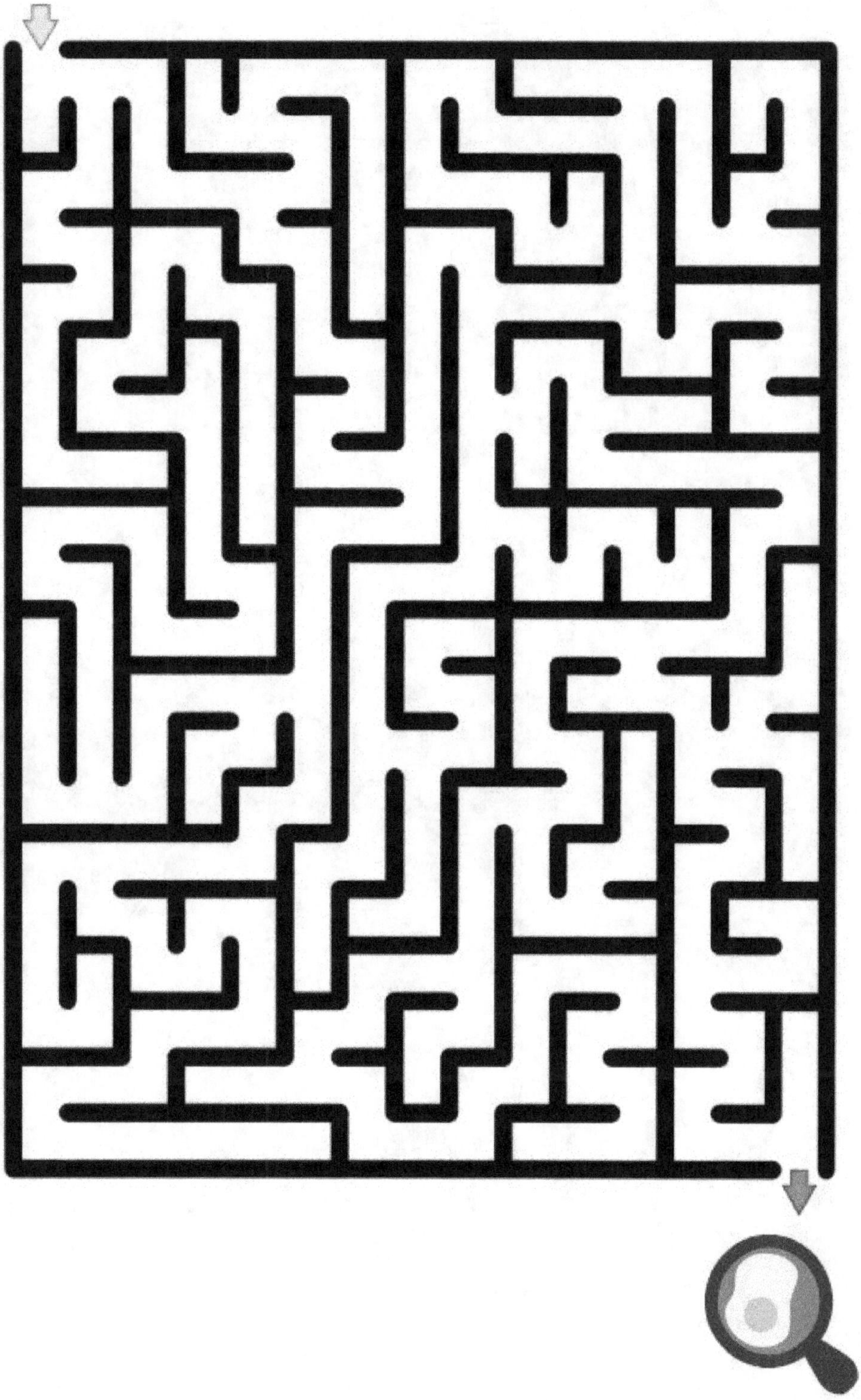

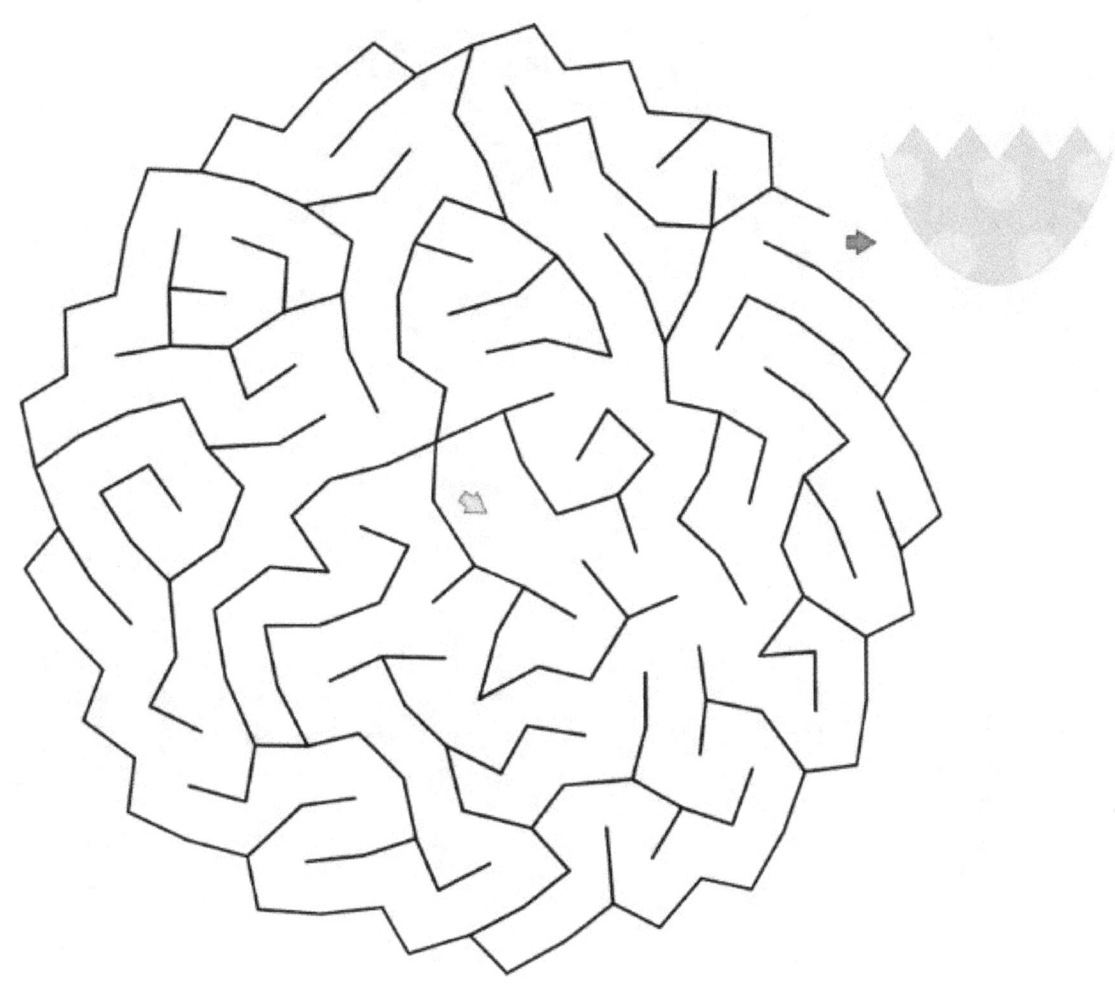

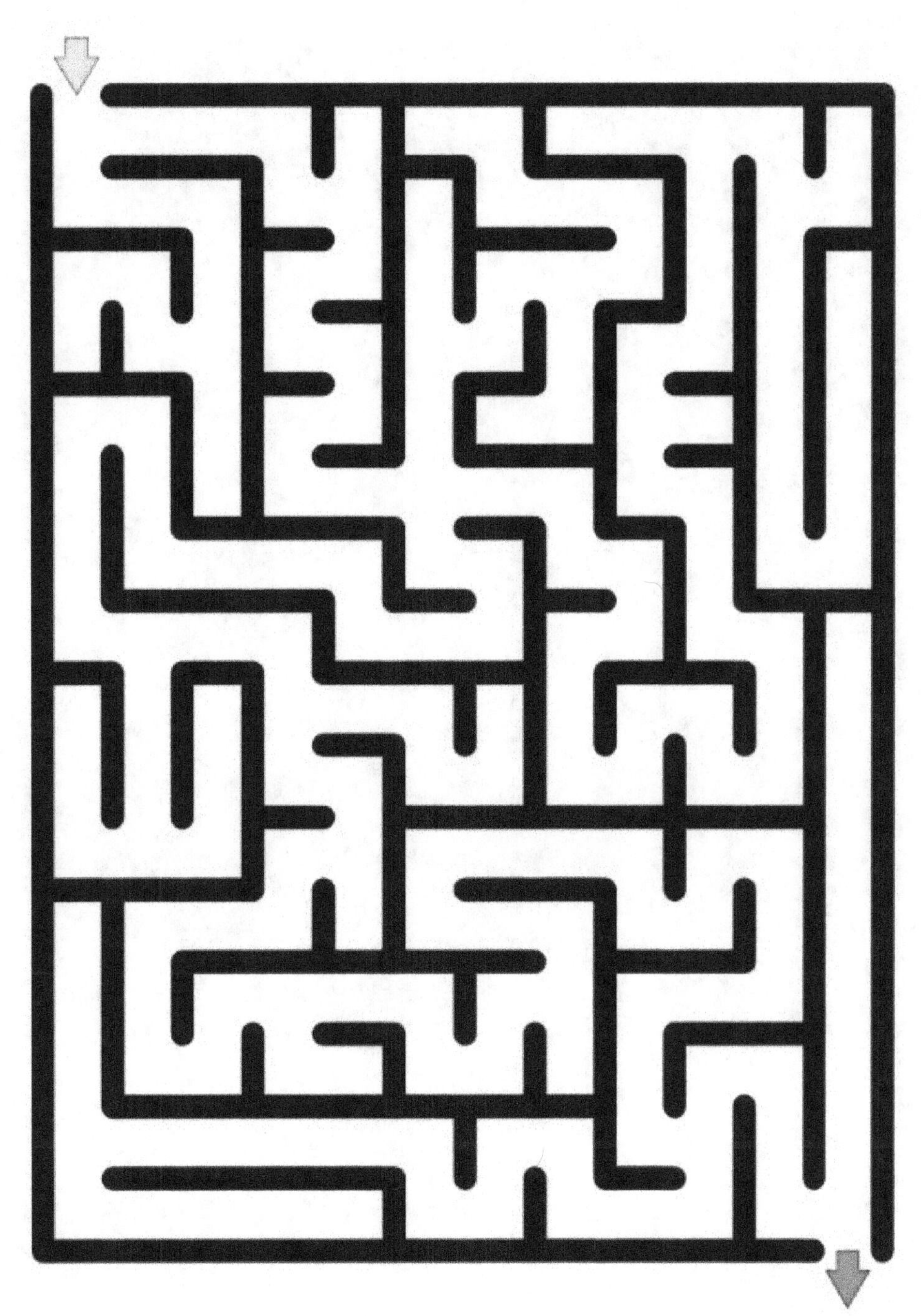

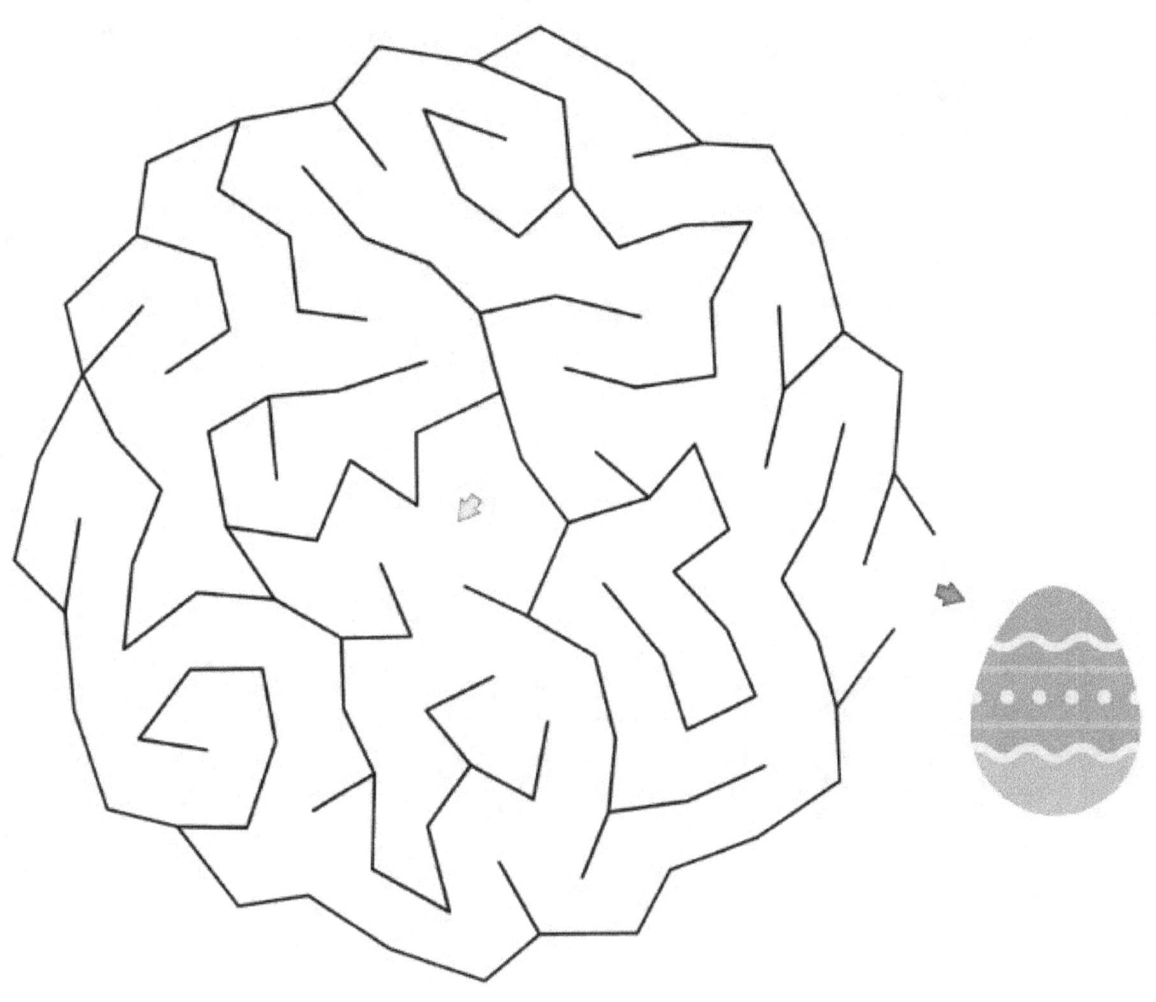

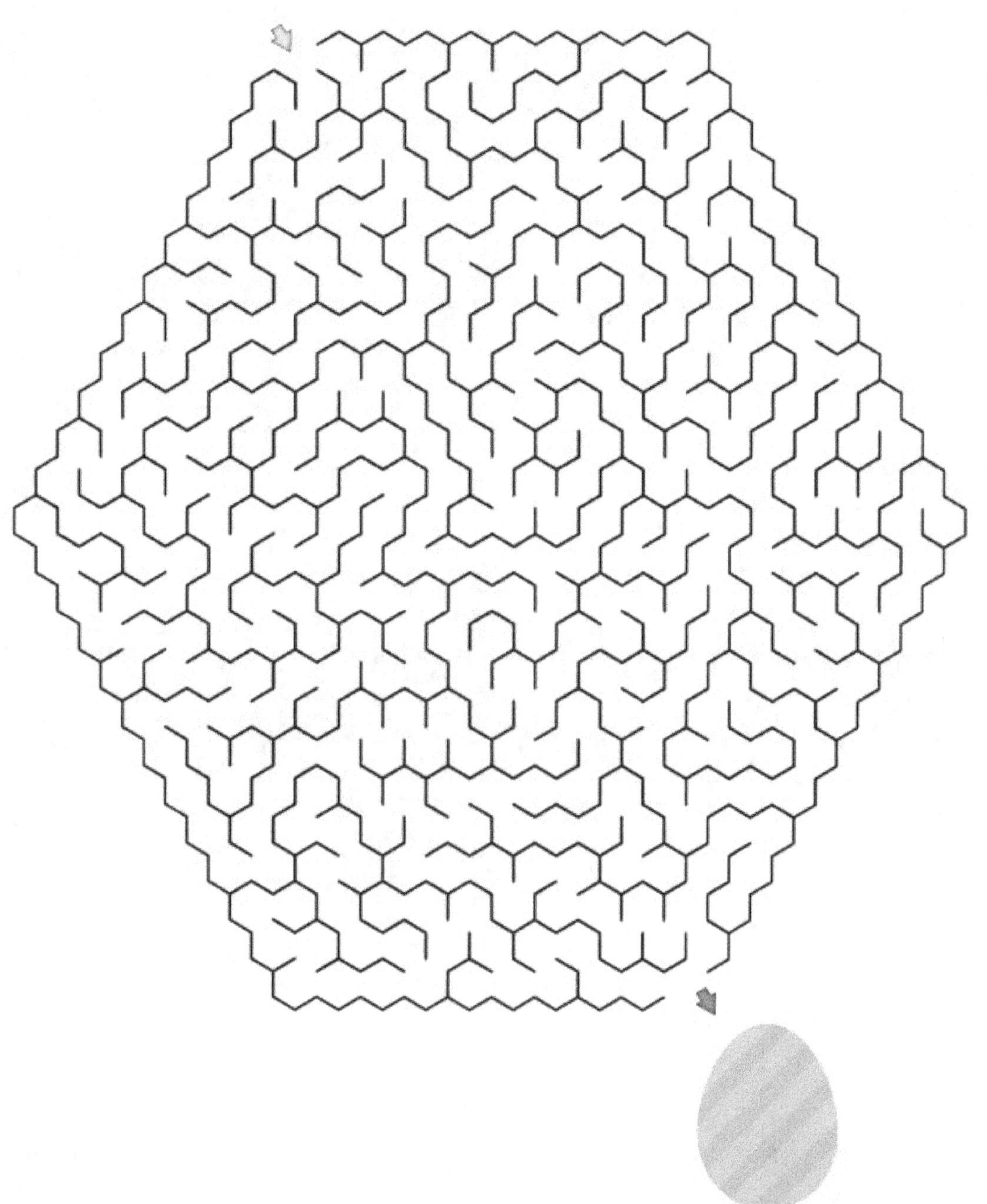

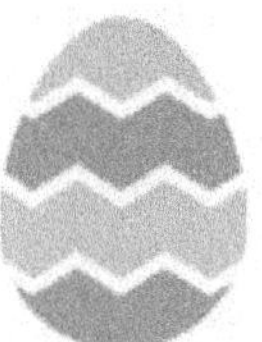

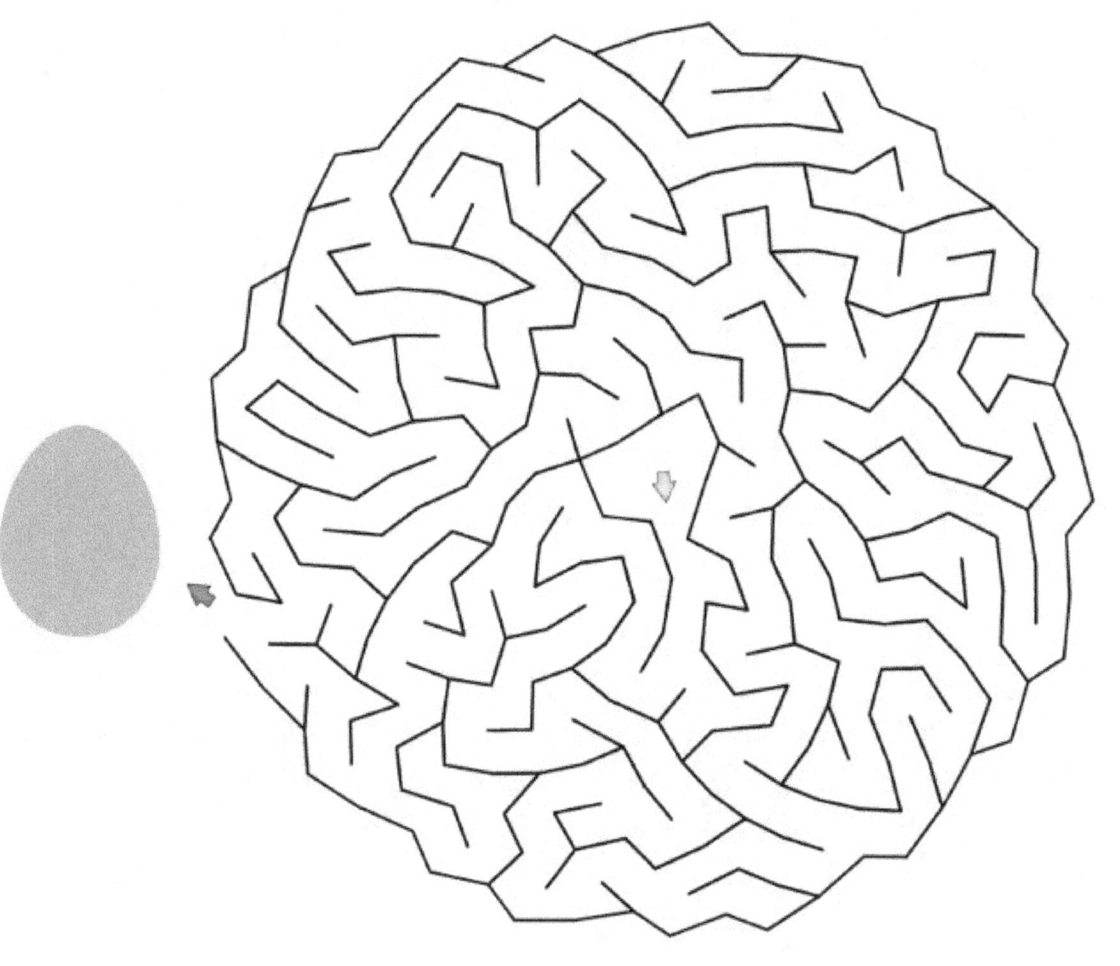